HORRIBLE SCIENCE

Really Rotten EXPERIMENTS

Nick Arnold
Tony De-Saulles

SCHOLASTIC

Scholastic Children's Books,
Euston House, 24 Eversholt Street
London NW1 1DB

A division of Scholastic Ltd
London ~ New York ~ Toronto ~ Sydney ~ Auckland
Mexico City ~ New Delhi ~ Hong Kong

First published in the UK by Scholastic Ltd, 2003

10 digit ISBN 0 439 97735 5
13 digit ISBN 978 0439 97735 7

Printed and bound in Finland by WS Bookwell

10 9 8 7

Contents

Introduction

Science is about discovery. It's about finding out facts and uncovering strange secrets.

And to help them, scientists have a secret weapon. It's called an "experiment". Thanks to experiments a scientist can tell you the answers to questions you haven't even thought of…

And answers you probably never wanted to know…

But why should experiments just be for serious-minded scientists? Surely they're far too much fun not to share around? Well, the good news is that now you can experience experiments for yourself!

And not just *any* old experiments either. This Horrible Science book is bulging with *rotten* experiments. *Really* rotten experiments. The sort of experiments that you should only try if you want to stagger a scientist or torture a teacher. Experiments that offer awesome answers to strange scientific secrets such as:

• How can water *walk*?

• What goes on in your stomach and why?

• How big does your bladder get?

• How can lizards walk up walls?

• And what happens when you put a teacher in the deep-freeze for a very long time?

Try them and I bet you'll have a really rotten time (and you'll enjoy every minute of it!). But be warned … you might find it hard to stop and then you could be in danger of turning into a scientist yourself!

A visit to Rotten Road ... and a warning!

Before we start this book, I'd like to say a great big word of thanks…

THANKS!

…to the pupils and teachers of Rotten Road School who agreed to test the experiments for this book. So let's go and meet them…

THE TEACHERS...

Mrs Cross is our head teacher. Mrs Cross is always cross but luckily we don't see much of her...

FUME!

SIGH!

Mr Bunsen is our teacher. He's a bit boring but he does come up with some cool experiments...

HAVE AN EXCITING DAY!

Miss Fitt is our classroom assistant. She helps us sometimes – when she's not eating...

MUNCH!

RIPPER

GROWL!

Mrs Gloop is our dinner lady. She's nearly as scary as Mrs Cross!

Beware of the dog....

Hisss!

SLASHER

...and the cat too!

DRIP!

Well, thanks for that, everyone, and now on with the experiments! Er – hold on, this book is being pulled over by a Science Safety Cop…

This book is about experiments but it's NOT about causing…

…cruelty to dumb animals, little brothers or family pets. There is some cruelty to teachers, but only in the interests of science and education (and having a good laugh).

ALSO, DON'T USE…
• Electricity – especially from the mains
• Boiling water
• Flames, matches or gas – and especially beware of all three put together

HERE'S WHAT HAPPENS IF YOU COMBINE A MATCH AND A FLAME WITH GAS.

Before you start experimenting, always read the instructions and make sure you've got everything you need. Many of the experiments in this book have been given a warning sign. Take time to find out what it means!

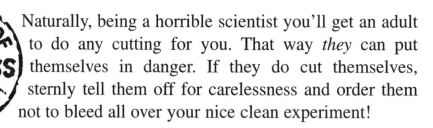

Naturally, being a horrible scientist you'll get an adult to do any cutting for you. That way *they* can put themselves in danger. If they do cut themselves, sternly tell them off for carelessness and order them not to bleed all over your nice clean experiment!

 Some adults are messy experimenters. This sign warns them about messy experiments that must be done on newspaper or outside and followed by immediate clearing-up operations. Naturally you were going to do this anyway – WEREN'T YOU?

 Look for the little sign next to it that tells you what the danger is. It's only kind to round up any nearby adults and warn them about the danger. That way they won't harm themselves when they try the experiment secretly after you've gone to bed.

 Adults get very grumpy if they can't do something – for this reason the trickier experiments have this warning. If you see this sign, make sure an adult's about so you can show them how easily you can do the experiment…

OK, YOU'RE ALLOWED TO READ ON NOW – HAVE A NICE DAY.

Phew! I reckon we got off lightly! But we'd best be careful, readers. The next chapter is about body experiments and they can be awfully *bloody…*

HAS ANYONE SEEN MY FINGER?

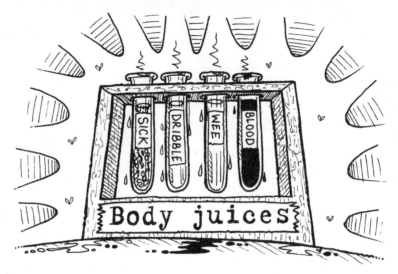

Bloody body experiments

You might think that your body is a walking, wobbling, skin-bag full of blood 'n' guts and mysterious bits 'n' pieces that you learnt about in science but can't remember the names of. And, of course, you'd be right! But your body is also full of foul fascinating scientific secrets. And because there are more than six billion living human bodies on Earth, it should be ever so easy to get your hands on one for your experiments … in fact you could even use your own!

And now let's pay another visit to Rotten Road School…

The Really Rotten Kids in… Belly-busters!

In this story, Mrs Gloop's famously foul school dinner does terrible things to Mr Bunsen's stomach – and Mr B isn't even around at the time!

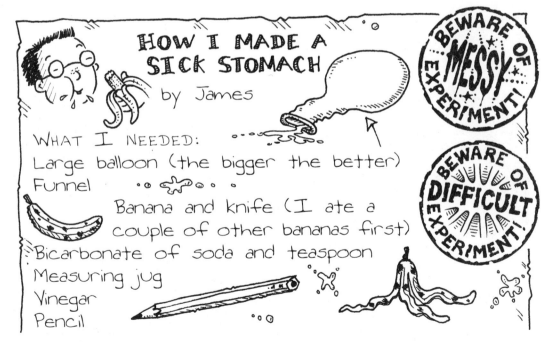

WHAT I DID:

1. I blew up the balloon a few times and let the air out until the balloon was saggy and baggy.

NEW BALLOON

SAG!

2. Next, I rolled the upper neck of the balloon over the neck of the funnel.

3. I chopped up a few small bits of banana and plopped them in the funnel. I used the end of the pencil to squish the banana into the balloon. The balloon wasn't as hungry as I was!

4. I squeezed the balloon a few times to squelch and squish and mash the banana. It felt gross!

5. After that I poured two teaspoonfuls of bicarbonate of soda into the balloon.

6. Then I poured 50 ml of vinegar into the balloon. I had to twist the balloon's neck tightly to stop anything getting out.

WHAT I FOUND:
The balloon stomach started fizzing and swelled up as gas formed inside it. When I let the gas out, the stomach burped. And when I squeezed the balloon, it sicked up half-digested banana everywhere. After that I felt sick and I didn't want any more banana.

The science behind the experiment

Digestion is how your guts break your food into chemicals to help your body grow and make energy.

1 A real stomach holds about 1.5 litres of food in a disgusting mashed-up mixture of slippery slimy spit-slobbered Brussels sprouts, gloopy gravy and snotty school custard. Tasteeee!

2 The teeth chew the food and the stomach churns and mashes up the mixture. When you mashed the banana inside the balloon, you were doing the stomach's job for it.

3 Like the vinegar you added to your balloon stomach, the real stomach makes an acid that dissolves the food into a gloopy soupy sloppy sludge.

4 Muscles called sphincters (s-vink-ters) hold the top and bottom openings of the stomach closed and stop you from sicking up your supper as your stomach squelches. Your balloon didn't have a sphincter and that's why you had to twist its neck instead.

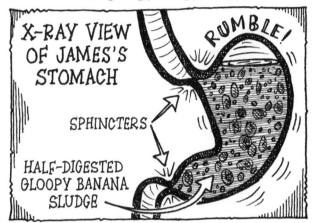

X-RAY VIEW OF JAMES'S STOMACH

RUMBLE!

SPHINCTERS

HALF-DIGESTED GLOOPY BANANA SLUDGE

5 Air can escape from the stomach as a burp. In the cartoon story, the indigestion pill worked like the bicarbonate of soda and vinegar. It made gas and the stomach swelled up.

6 When you're sick, the muscles around your stomach squeeze just like your hand squeezing the balloon. And, just as in the experiment, they squeeze so hard that the squirting sick splatters out. So keep a safe distance from sicky little brothers or sisters!

The Really Rotten Kids in… Toilet tortures

Have you ever wanted to go the toilet during a lesson? That's how James is feeling right now! He drank too much fizzy pop at lunchtime – and now he's *really* suffering!

But what's happening *inside* him?

And what will Mr Bunsen say if James sticks up his hand?

Bet you never knew!

Your pee is stored in your bladder. But when you feel nervous, the stretchy sides of your bladder can go stiff and stop stretching. Your bladder feels full. And that's why you have to trot to the toilet – or even leap for the lavatory in an extreme emergency.

And now here's your chance to find out what's *really* going on down below…

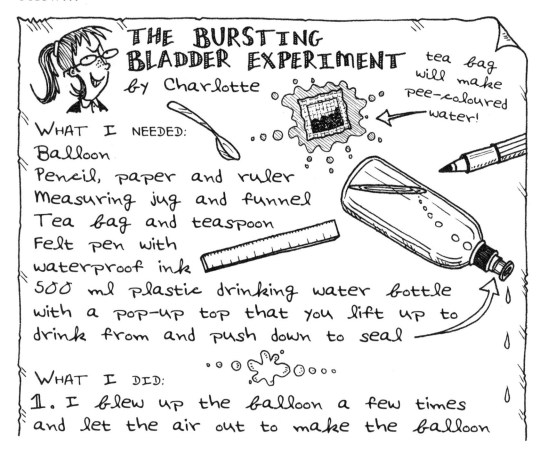

more stretchy. I measured the size of the balloon across and wrote it on the piece of paper.

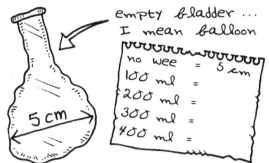

empty bladder ...
I mean balloon

no wee = 5 cm
100 ml =
200 ml =
300 ml =
400 ml =

5 cm

2. I filled the measuring jug with 400 ml of water. I placed the tea bag in the water and pushed it about with the teaspoon until the water was the colour of pee. Then I threw the tea bag away.

WEE!

3. Next, I poured 100 ml of water into the bottle through the funnel. I held the bottle upside down and marked the water level 100 ml on the outside of the bottle.

4. I repeated step three for 200, 300 and 400 ml and that's how I could tell how much water was in the bottle.

5. Then I rolled the neck of the balloon over the top of the bottle so it made a nice tight fit. I held the bottle upside down and squeezed 100 ml of water into the balloon. Then I measured the size of the balloon across and wrote it down.

6. I carried on filling the balloon in 100-ml stages until it held 400 ml of water.

WHAT I FOUND:
The balloon swelled up and changed shape as more pee went into it. Afterwards I emptied the balloon into the sink.
Oh yuck! It looked like someone had peed in there!

The science behind the experiment

1 Pee is mostly water that's been filtered out of the blood by the kidneys.

2 Tea and coffee make you go to the toilet more often. They contain a substance called caffeine (caff-een) that widens the blood vessels. This means more blood zips to your kidneys and so more water ends up being squirted down to your bladder.

3 But even when your kidneys are working at their usual speed, every minute they squirt 1.4 ml of pee to the bladder and this can have embarrassing results…

Let's imagine you're sitting in a science lesson … it looks like you're paying attention, but deep inside your bladder is filling up with all that lovely lemonade you swigged at lunchtime…

100 ml You're feeling a bit uncomfortable. Hmm – maybe I should have gone to the toilet before the lesson started, you think.

200 ml You're feeling more discomfort. Shall I put my hand up? you wonder. Deep inside, your bladder is filling up and it's turning from a little wrinkly prune-like bag into a bloated bulging balloon up to 10 cm across.

300 ml You feel like getting up and dancing. So you put up your hand and your teacher says… NO – YOU'LL HAVE TO WAIT!

400 ml Let's hope the teacher changes her mind or you'll be needing a bucket and a mop! SPLISH! SPLOSH!

The Really Rotten Kids in… Hello, hot-lips!

Mr Bunsen discovers someone's been drinking out of his new mug and his secret bun supply is disappearing. There's going to be trouble, and the science of lips and teeth offers the only solution…

HOW I TESTED LIP- AND TEETH-PRINTS
by Katie

WHAT I NEEDED:
Some lipstick (it took me ages to find the right colour!)
A piece of paper
A rolling pin
A piece of plasticine or Blu-Tack

OOH, LOVELY!

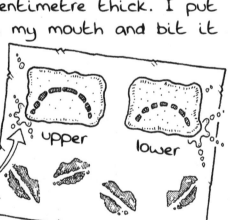

WHAT I DID:

1. I put a little lipstick on my lovely lips.

2. Then I lightly pressed my lips on the paper.

3. Using the rolling pin, I rolled the plasticine so it was about half a centimetre thick. I put the sheet of plasticine in my mouth and bit it – but not too hard.

4. I could see my lip-prints on the paper and the plasticine showed the shape of my upper and lower teeth.

dribble

upper   lower

WHAT I FOUND:

1. My lip- and teeth-prints looked different from Charlotte's. Of course, mine looked far nicer!

2. Sam did this experiment and nearly ate the plasticine – he got green bits stuck between his teeth. THIS IS WRONG!

The science behind the experiment

1 No one's got lips like yours. And that means everyone makes different lip-prints. Like fingerprints, they're unique to that person.

2 Here are some lip-print patterns to look out for…

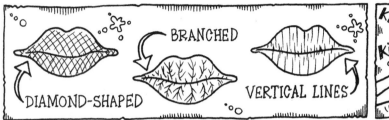 

3 Teeth patterns are unique too. They depend on…

• How many teeth you have.

• How big your teeth are.

• How they're growing. Some teeth grow at wonky angles.

4 We've borrowed Mrs Cross's false teeth to show you what different teeth do…

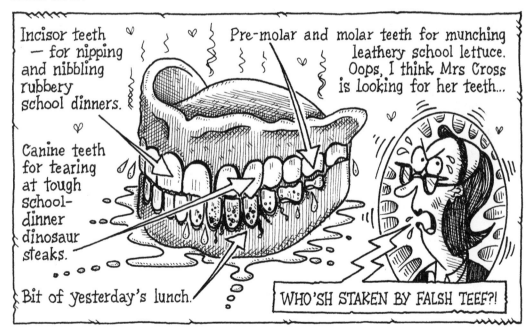

The Really Rotten Kids in… A sting in the tale

Are you good at staying still, or are you always fidgeting? And is it humanly possible for anyone to stay completely still? Mr Bunsen thinks he knows the answer…

If Thomas hadn't tripped, Mr Bunsen might have been able to stay still for hours or even days. But muscles are never completely still, as Nathan is about to find out…

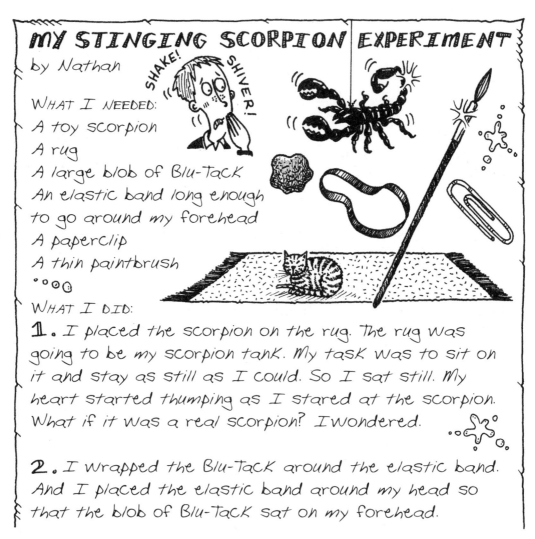

MY STINGING SCORPION EXPERIMENT

by Nathan

WHAT I NEEDED:

A toy scorpion

A rug

A large blob of Blu-Tack

An elastic band long enough to go around my forehead

A paperclip

A thin paintbrush

WHAT I DID:

1. I placed the scorpion on the rug. The rug was going to be my scorpion tank. My task was to sit on it and stay as still as I could. So I sat still. My heart started thumping as I stared at the scorpion. What if it was a real scorpion? I wondered.

2. I wrapped the Blu-Tack around the elastic band. And I placed the elastic band around my head so that the blob of Blu-Tack sat on my forehead.

3. Next, I placed the paperclip on the paintbrush handle. Then I stuck the paintbrush into the Blu-Tack so that it stuck out of my forehead.

WOBBLE!

It was a stressful business

4. I tried to hold the handle of the paintbrush steady so that the paperclip didn't move.

WHAT I FOUND:
The paperclip soon started to wobble. Aaargh! That meant I was moving. If I moved too much, I could get stung by the scorpion!* Luckily, at that moment, the dog came and grabbed the scorpion and ran off with it. You saved my life, Buster!

*NOTE TO NERVOUS READERS...
Don't panic! Nathan was only twitching. And you probably WON'T be stung by a scorpion just because you twitched!

The science behind the experiment

Even when you think you're being completely still, your body makes tiny movements. Your eyes are blinking and your muscles are twitching, although you might not want them to. Even the blood pulsing through your blood vessels can send tiny shockwaves through your body.

Bet you never knew!
People really do sit in tanks with live scorpions. In 2001, Malena Hasum of Malaysia spent 30 days with 2,700 scorpions, and the following year, Kanchana Katkaew shared a tank in Thailand for 32 days with 3,400 scuttling, stinging thingies. After that I bet she needed a good run around!

The Really Rotten Kids in… Bad taste

Take a quick peek at the front cover of this book. Some Rotten Road kids are trying a tasteless experiment on Mr Bunsen. But did they really go this far? Surely not! Well you can find out what really happened in a few seconds. But now for a fact that you might find hard to swallow…

Bet you never knew!

If two people share the same food, each person will probably find it tastes slightly different. That's because everyone's spit has a slightly different taste – for example, some spit is a little more salty. And the slurpy spit adds to the flavour of the food. That means if you spat on someone's food and they ate it, it would taste different to them. Er, don't try this experiment at home – or at school!

HOW I FOUND OUT ABOUT TASTELESS FOOD
by James

IS THIS WISE? I ASK MYSELF

BEWARE OF CARELESS CUTTING!

WHAT I NEEDED:
A blindfold (a strip of cloth was all I needed)
Mr Bunsen (I could have experimented on my friends)
Two small pieces of potato (chopped up by Mrs Gloop)
A big glass of water
Two small pieces of apple (also chopped up by Mrs Gloop)
Some small glasses of blackcurrant squash, orange squash and lemon juice

WHAT I DID:
1. I blindfolded Mr Bunsen and made him hold his nose.

2. I asked Mr Bunsen to eat a piece of potato. Then I asked him whether he thought it was an apple or a potato. He said it was an apple! Mr Bunsen then had to swill out his mouth with water to get rid of the taste.

3. When I gave Mr Bunsen a piece of apple, he thought it was a potato!

I gave Mr Bunsen the other piece of apple and then the other piece of potato but this time I let him sniff the food as he ate. He was able to tell which food was which.

4. Mr Bunsen had to hold his nose as he sipped the blackcurrant squash. After he slurped some water, he held his nose again. This time he had a drink of orange squash. He couldn't tell the difference between the orange and the blackcurrant.

5. Then I made him drink the lemon juice. He could tell what it was even when he was holding his nose...

WHAT I FOUND:
1. Most of the time you need to sniff and taste food to find out what it is.

2. Lemon juice tastes really sour - I know, because I tried it too. YUCK! Mr Bunsen's tongue can detect this taste without any help from his nose.

3. Afterwards Charlotte, Hannah, Thomas and Matt gave Mr Bunsen some more horrible food. That was nothing to do with me - mind you, it was really funny. Especially when Mr Bunsen turned green and started making gagging sounds!

The science behind the experiment

1 Most of the time when you think you're tasting your food, you're actually *smelling* it. Your sense of taste detects chemicals dissolved by the slimy spit on your tingling tongue. Sniffing checks out whiffy chemicals wafting up your nose from your food.

2 Your sense of smell is about TEN THOUSAND times more sensitive than your sense of taste. This explains why it's hard to know what foods are when you can't sniff them.

3 It also explains why trying to eat with a cold is like chewing crunchy cardboard.

4 When you sniff food, you're likely to drool and the wet dribble on your tongue helps you to taste the food more easily. When you can't smell the food before you eat it, you don't make so much spit. And this makes the food harder to taste.

5 Different parts of the tongue can detect different tastes. But, oddly enough, the middle of the tongue isn't too good at tasting.

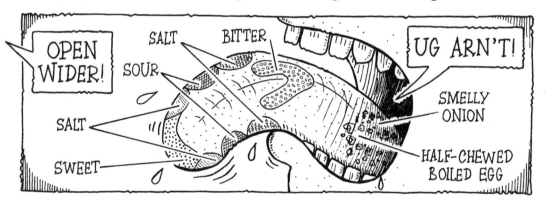

I expect the lemon juice sent Mr Bunsen's sour-spotting areas into overdrive…

Now, to end this chapter on a suitably nasty note, here's the first of a series of really rotten quizzes… Have *you* got the guts to read on…?

Queasy quiz 1

Feeling queasy? You will be! Which of the following are real body experiments and which are made up because they're too terrible to be true?

1 Preserving a dead body in plastic.

2 Preserving a dead body in custard.

3 Listening to music to prevent colds.

4 Discovering whether red-haired girls feel more pain than other girls.

5 Comparing the brains of teachers and chimpanzees.

Answers:

1 TRUE. German scientist Gunther von Hagens invented the method in 1978 and he went on to create an eerie exhibition featuring real chopped-up dead bodies and brains and livers and lungs in tasteful poses.

2 FALSE. As far as I know, no one's ever found a complete body in school-dinner custard … *yet!*

3 TRUE. In 1998, US scientists showed that your body churns out more of a germ-fighting substance when it's happy. And it's happy when it's listening to music. So the volunteers made mucus to music. Yes, they listened … and they spat. Scientists scooped up the spit and measured the germ-fighting chemicals in the globs of slimy slobber.

4 TRUE. In 2002, scientists in Kentucky, USA, found that red-haired girls feel more pain than blonde or dark-haired girls. The scientists gave the girls mild electric shocks. But don't get any ideas, it's unkind to wire up your little sister to the Christmas tree!

5 FALSE. As everyone knows, a chimp is *far* superior – er, I mean *inferior* – to a teacher.

And if you're smarter than the average ape, you'll want to read on because we'll be looking at brains in the next chapter…

Baffling brain experiments

We've given the brain its very own chapter because it's a very important body bit…

For starters, you need a brain to help you read this book. And if you didn't have a brain, your science homework wouldn't just be hard – it would be impossible!

Anyway, why not forget about homework and read this chilling chapter? It's easy on the brain and you're sure to get your head round it. And it won't give you too many headaches… (Message from the editor: That's enough brain jokes for now!)

The Really Rotten Kids in… Let's face it

Rebecca is an arty type and now she's come up with the scariest Halloween idea ever. It's so scary, Mr Bunsen is about to get the shock of his life…

Here are some good scientific reasons why Mr Bunsen is shocked by the face picture:

1 He's taken by surprise.

2 The face is scary for reasons you're about to find out.

3 Mr B's brain is wired up to take a special interest in faces.

Bet you never knew!

Your brain is always looking for faces and that's why you notice them in odd places. You might spot faces in clouds or patterns of slime on your mouldy classroom wall. In 1976, some astonished astronomers even reckoned they saw an alien face in a mountain on Mars.

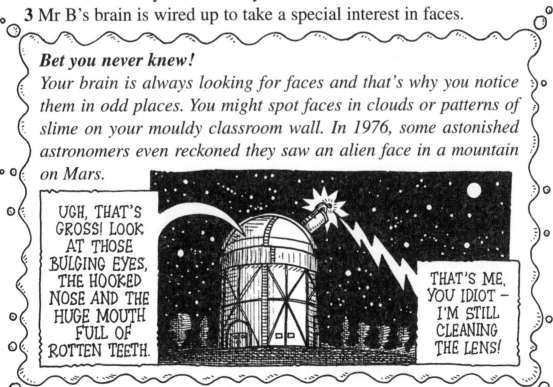

And now to check out what made Rebecca's face picture so scary…

HOW I MADE A HORRIBLE FACE
by Rebecca

BEWARE OF CARELESS CUTTING!

WHAT I NEEDED:

A big photo of a face (I used one of me, and my mum made it bigger on a photocopier. I could have cut the face out of a magazine - but dad was still reading it!)

A mirror

Scissors

Some glue

A piece of paper the same size as the photo

A friend

GLOO

WHAT I DID:

1. I placed the mirror lengthways over the photo of the face like so...

I looked at this side...

mirror

2. I cut out the eyes and mouth like so...

3. I glued the photo of the face on to another piece of paper. Then I glued the eyes and the mouth back in their proper places - except they were upside down.

4. I held the face upside down and asked Katie to look at it.

WHAT I FOUND:

1. When the left side of the face was reflected in the mirror, the face looked strange and a bit scary.

2. When the eyes and mouth were upside down and the face was the right way up, the face looked even more scary!

3. But when Katie saw the face upside down, she didn't find it scary at all! She said it looked normal!

The science behind the experiment

1 The brain is divided into two halves joined in the middle. In most people the left side of the brain deals with facts and maths, and the right side of the brain looks after feelings and artistic, touchy-feely stuff.

2 Now imagine you're looking at someone's face. Your brain makes a picture in your mind from the information sent by your eyes. But each half of the face you're looking at is dealt with by a separate half of your brain. Hmm – don't know about you, but *both* sides of my brain are baffled by this. Let's see if this diagram helps…

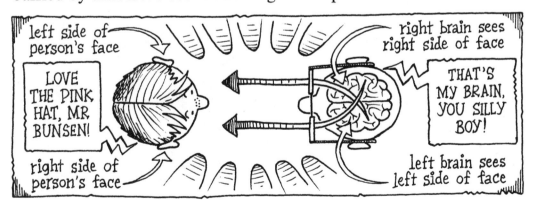

3 Although the left brain is very smart, it isn't too clever at judging faces and feelings. In stage **1** Rebecca was using her left brain to look at her face – and that's why it looked odd to her.

31

4 Your brain is wired up to remember faces. The bits of the face that show most feelings are the eyes and the mouth, and these are the bits that the brain pays most attention to. If the eyes and the mouth look wrong, the whole face looks horrible. If the eyes and the mouth look OK, the rest of the face can be upside down but the brain still thinks the face looks normal. And I bet you never knew that looking at someone was so complicated!

The Really Rotten Kids in… Mask madness

And talking about faces – here are two horrible heads. Which one does strange things to your brain?

No, it's NOT Mrs Cross! When you turn the mask to face the wall, something weird happens in your head. Find out what this is by trying the experiment yourself…

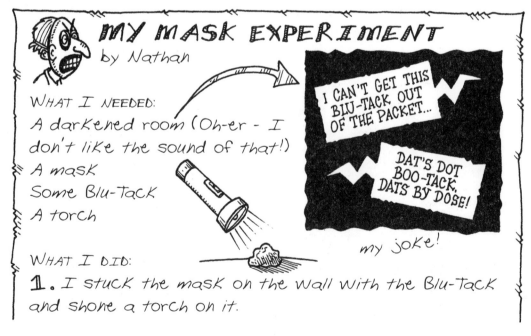

2. It looked just like a scary face sticking out of the wall. Er ... I'm getting a bad feeling about this!

3. Then I turned the mask around to face the wall, so the face would disappear.

4. I shone the torch on it again and... ARGGGH!

WHAT I FOUND:
YIKES! The mask still looked as if it was facing outwards. Maybe it turned around on its own? ... Perhaps it's ALIVE?! I'm outta here!

The science behind the experiment

1 Remember how the brain is geared up to recognize faces? Well, that's fine as long as the face is the right way round.

2 But the brain isn't so good at making sense of sights it's not used to seeing. So the brain "sees" the back-to-front face as being the right way round.

Bet you never knew!
When you look at something, your eye doesn't make sense of it – your brain does! That means when you look at this dog, your eye sees a doggie shape...
And your brain puts all the info together and matches it up with your memory of a dog and says...

GRRR!

YIKES - IT'S RIPPER! I'M OUTTA HERE!

The Really Rotten Kids in… Tricky flickers

An educational tour of a cinema turns into a nightmare for Mr Bunsen. But at least he tells the kids what films do to their brains!

WHAT I DID:

1. My mum photocopied the cartoons on the next page. She had to photocopy them on a piece of thin card. I could have traced them or even drawn them myself...

2. I cut out each of the cartoon boxes and put them in a pile. These were the pages of my flicker book. Cartoon number 1 was on top and number 16 was at the bottom.

3. I used the two paperclips to hold the pages together.

paper clips

4. I flicked through the book I'd made...

WHAT I FOUND:

WOW! I saw a mini-movie of Mr Bunsen getting a bowl of Mrs Gloop's custard poured over his head. I showed it to everyone at school and they thought it was wicked! But then Mr Bunsen saw it and he gave me extra science homework as a punishment.

The science behind the experiment

1 Mr Bunsen's already explained the scientific basics in the cartoon story.

2 When you see a film, your brain takes in the whole scene and then tries to makes sense of what's going on.

3 But, as Mr Bunsen said, everything's moving so fast that the brain sees a single moving picture rather than thousands of separate pictures.

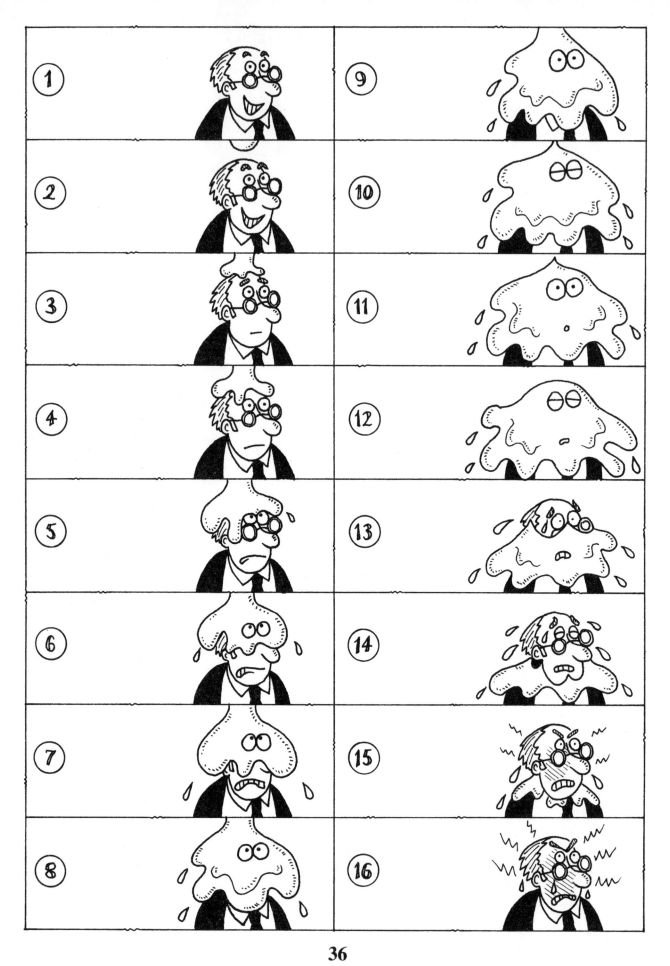

The Really Rotten Kids in… Double trouble

Besides making sense of movement, your brain is brilliant at judging distances. And that's how you can see in three dimensions (3-D).

I KNOW A REALLY NEAT TRICK…

COOL!

I PAINT BUNS ON YOUR GLASSES…

IF I PAINT A SLIGHTLY DIFFERENT BUN ON EACH LENS…

…YOUR BRAIN PUTS THEM TOGETHER TO SEE A 3-D BUN FLOATING IN MID-AIR!

WISH I COULD EAT IT!

Bet you never knew!

Your brain actually receives two pictures of the outside world – one from each eyeball. The fact that you only see one picture is thanks to your brain blending the pictures together. When the brain can't manage this job it's called "seeing double".

HOW I MADE A 3-D MONSTER
by Rebecca

WHAT I NEEDED:
My eyes
A4 card
A4 paper
Scissors

BEWARE OF CARELESS CUTTING!

WHAT I DID:

1. I drew two cartoons of Mrs Cross and Mum photocopied them.

2. Then I cut out the cartoon copies and set up the experiment...

A

B

3. With my nose on the edge of the card, I could see cartoon A through my left eye but not through my right.

Cartoon A

A4 card on its side along dotted line

Paper

4. I relaxed my eyes as if looking at the distance. A second cartoon appeared to the right of cartoon A. I put cartoon B over it (I had to lift the A4 card a little.)

WHAT I FOUND:

The two cartoons blended together. I saw a 3-D Mrs Cross! She looked scary and real. It was really neat!

The science behind the experiment

1 When you look at the two drawings, your brain is hard at work doing what it always does. It's putting together slightly different views of the same scene to make one 3-D picture. The two slightly different views are normally what you see with each eyeball.

2 There's a big overlap between what we see with each eye. This is called "binocular vision". By turning this overlap into a 3-D view, your brilliant brain gives you a sense of depth and helps you to judge distances. Clever – huh?

Bet you never knew!

There's a big difference between rabbits and humans. And it's not because rabbits munch their own poo and we don't. (This is a big difference but it wasn't the one I was thinking of.)

Rabbits have eyes on the sides of their heads and we have them in front. A rabbit can see through a wide angle but there's not much overlap between what its eyes see. And that means rabbits don't have 3-D vision.

The Really Rotten Kids in… Mirror muddle

Mirrors can do strange things to your brain. And they can also do strange things to science tests, as Mr Bunsen is about to discover…

THIS MIRROR WILL ADD A TOUCH OF CLASS TO THE CLASSROOM.

OOH, LOVELY!

LATER… WE'VE GOT A SCIENCE TEST!

GROAN!

DURING THE TEST…

PSST! YOU CAN SEE THE ANSWERS IN THE MIRROR!

WHAT THEY SEE…

WORD SOON GETS AROUND, AND BEFORE LONG…

FINISHED!

B-B-BUT THAT'S IMPOSSIBLE!

THEY'RE WRITTEN BACK TO FRONT. HMM — MIRRORS REFLECT BACK TO FRONT. I SMELL A RAT!

THE NEXT DAY… LOOK IN THE MIRROR, KIDS…

WHAT THEY SEE…

TODAY'S WORK: EXTRA SCIENCE TEST

SIGH!

HOW I DREW IN THE MIRROR
by Katie

BEAUTIFUL!

WHAT I NEEDED:

The monster maze on the next page
A mirror
A pencil
A piece of A4 paper cut in half lengthways
An elastic band long enough to stretch around my forehead
A felt pen

WHAT I DID:

1. I got my mum to photocopy the maze drawing. I would have traced it but that's too much like hard work.

2. I propped the mirror upright and, looking in it, I tried to guide my pencil along the maze.

3. Next, I tied back my lovely hair and wrapped the paper around my forehead and secured it with the elastic band.

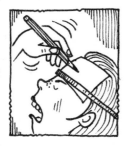 4. I took the felt pen and closed my eyes and tried to imagine my hand writing my first name in capital letters on a piece of paper. I wrote quickly without thinking about what I was doing – it's lucky I'm a quick writer!

5. I looked at myself in the mirror. "WOW! That's amazing!" I gasped. No, I wasn't admiring my lovely looks – I was looking at what I had written!

WHAT I FOUND:

1. The maze was really hard and I kept going the wrong way and nearly getting caught by the monsters.

2. But when I wrote on my forehead, I found I had written my name in mirror writing without thinking!

The only problem is I can't stop doing it!

The science behind the experiment

1 A mirror reflects light, but it reflects light coming from the left to the right. And it sends the light from the right off to the left. This means that when you look in the mirror, you see left and right reversed. See what I mean?

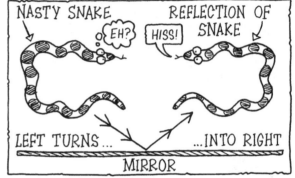

NASTY SNAKE   REFLECTION OF SNAKE
EH? HISS!
LEFT TURNS...   ...INTO RIGHT
MIRROR

2 Your poor old brain finds this very confusing, especially when it's trying to give orders to the hand holding the pen.

WHICH WAY DO I GO?

DON'T ASK ME, I'M LOST!

3 You're used to writing your name, aren't you? You can do it so easily that you can even do it without thinking! In fact, that's exactly what happens in the forehead-writing part of the experiment.

4 There's a part of your brain called the cerebellum (ser-re-bell-um) that controls movements you know so well that you don't have to think about them. But there's a problem. Your cerebellum only knows what to do when your hand is facing *forwards*. When you write on your bonce, your hand is facing the opposite way and that means your name comes out *backwards*. That's right – it's mirror writing!

The Really Rotten Kids in… Cockroach cocktails

This experiment is all about the faces people make – especially the kind of disgusted face you're pulling as you read this disgusting book. Mr Bunsen is about to enjoy a nice glass of apple juice. Unfortunately, he hasn't noticed the dead cockroach in the drink.

Bet you never knew!

1 You can pull different faces because your face has dozens of muscles to help you. For example…

- *Two pairs of muscles widen and close your nostrils.*
- *Four pairs of muscles control your jaws.*
- *Seven pairs of muscles help you pucker up your lips.*

2 All in all, scientists reckon your face can make 7,000 different expressions. In a rare burst of energy, even dozy Sam managed a few that differed from his usual blank stare.

HOW I MADE A DISGUSTING DRINK
by Thomas

WHAT I NEEDED:
Some apple juice
A glass
Two friends
A cockroach (from a joke or toy shop)

WHAT I DID:
1. I poured apple juice into a glass.

2. I plopped the cockroach into the drink.

3. I offered the drink to Matt and James and watched their faces.

ERK!

WHAT I FOUND:
1. They both screwed up their faces in disgust. Actually, it didn't matter what I put in the apple juice. I tried it with a toy worm, and a really cool glow-in-the-dark toy spider. No one would touch the drink! Then I put the worm and the spider and the cockroach in the same drink...

2. And my little brother drank it.

SLURP!

ARGH!
THAT'S GROSS!

BEWARE OF DANGER!

Put a straw in the drink first and make sure little kids don't drink the bugs!

The science behind the experiment

1 You sense feelings in your brain and although feelings can feel pretty mushy and mixed up, scientists reckon you have six main feelings. Each feeling shows itself in the look on your face. Just watch the faces of these Rotten Road pupils…

a) Surprise

Followed by **b)** Happiness

Followed by **c)** Anger

Followed by **d)** Sadness

Followed by **e)** Fear

Followed by **f)** Disgust

2 Scientists from the Institute of Psychiatry have found everyone makes the same face when they feel disgust. They found this out by showing people photos of blocked toilets.

3 The cockroach experiment was inspired by the experiments of US scientist Paul Rozin. He offered children poo to eat and a cockroach in a glass of apple juice to drink. All the children turned him down in disgust, but a baby actually *ate* the poo! Luckily the "poo" turned out to be a rather yummy chocolate fudge cake. Would you risk a nibble?

4 Paul's experiment showed that children only learn that food can be disgusting when they're about three. Hmm – funny that, I always thought it was their first taste of school dinners!

Queasy quiz 2

Is your brain still buzzing? Here's your chance to discover if you have the brain of a brilliant boffin or a bamboozled budgerigar. The questions feature real experiments – but can your brain work out the answers?

1 In 2000, a man dressed as a football supporter pretended to be injured. What happened next?

a) No one helped him.
b) Supporters of all teams rushed to his aid.
c) He was only helped by supporters of his own side.

2 In 2001, a scientist tried a memory test designed for a chimp. What happened next?
a) The chimp attacked the scientist and stuffed a banana in her mouth so she couldn't answer the questions.
b) The scientist beat the chimp.
c) The chimp beat the scientist.

3 Why was a scientist looking at joke books in 2002?
a) Because he was bored.
b) He was looking for the world's WORST joke!
c) He wanted to find out why jokes make people laugh.

4 A scientist wired up a lime jelly to a brainwave-recording machine. What did he find?
a) The lime jelly was definitely dead.
b) The lime jelly wobbled whenever anyone talked to it.
c) The machine showed the lime jelly was *alive*!

5 A scientist spent two years trying to find out what made toddlers scream with laughter. What made the toddlers laugh?
a) The toddlers laughed for no reason.
b) Shouting the word "STINKY-POO!"
c) Both **a)** and **b)** and just about anything else too.

Answers:
ALL the answers are **c)** so you can work out your score without taxing your brain too much.
1 c) Liverpool supporters won't help anyone wearing a Manchester United shirt. Can you believe it?!
2 c) Scientist Susan Blackmore scored less on a number memory test than a chimp who lived in Japan.
3 c) Graeme Ritchie was trying to find out if jokes stay funny if you change the word order. So let's try it…

Yep, I'd agree that the joke was certainly funnier first time round. Mind you, it wasn't *that* funny even then.

4 c) Yes, the lime jelly lived! Well, according to the machine it did. In fact, Adrian Upton of Ontario, Canada, found the jelly was picking up noises from the next room – so you can pick up half a point for **b)** too.

5 c) So you can have a point for **a)** or **b)** too because I want to make you happy. Toddlers squeal with laugher when their teacher has an accident – so would you smile if your teacher slipped on a wet fish and landed with his head on a bucket of worms?

Well, talking about squealing, the next chapter's sure to squeeze a few squeaks out of YOU. You'll adore the animals, and the jokes will have you howling (hopefully) as you learn to make friends with your cat and other beasties…

Wicked wildlife experiments

Ah! The great outdoors! A breath of fresh air and the not-so-nice bits such as the stink of dung and the wailing whine of millions of maddening mosquitoes. Well, I suppose nature's only natural and, for an animal, it's home. So let's get out and about and visit our furry friends and hope they don't bite too badly…

Has anyone seen my suit of armour?

The Really Rotten Kids in… Little squirts

You might think that fish are boring, finny thingies that drift about letting out little bubbles. Well yes they are, but some fish are fairly freaky too. And Mr Bunsen is about to get up close and personal with one of the finest, funniest, finniest fish.

GROTTYVILLE PET SHOP PRESENTS…
Archer Fish
THESE INCREDIBLE FISH KNOCK DOWN INSECTS WITH SQUIRTS OF WATER — THEY'LL KEEP YOU AMUSED FOR HOURS!

THE KIDS ARE ON A VISIT TO THE PET SHOP...

PLEASE CAN WE GET SOME ARCHER FISH?!

OH, VERY WELL.

BACK AT SCHOOL...

GRRR — YOU LITTLE SQUIRTS!

HOW I BECAME A CHAMPION ARCHER FISH

by Chloë

WHAT I NEEDED:
Some thread, 90 cm long
A stick
A toy fly. I could have drawn a fly on a piece of card 1.5 cm square and cut it out.
A friend
A tape measure
A water pistol, or I could have used a clean, empty washing-up bottle full of water.

HOW I COULD HAVE MADE THE FLY

THREAD GOES THROUGH HOLE IN CARD

THREAD

KNOT

SMALL PIECE OF CARD WITH DRAWING OF A FLY →

BEWARE OF MESSY EXPERIMENT!

WHAT I DID:
1. I tied one end of the thread to the stick and the other to the fly.

2. Hannah held the stick for me.

3. I measured 2 metres from the fly and tried to squirt the fly from this range. I didn't think it would be too difficult — an archer fish can do it!

EEK!

2 METRES

SQUIRT!

Oops — I squirted Hannah by mistake!

WHAT I FOUND:

1. Hannah and I took it in turns to try the experiment and the room got a bit wet. And then we remembered that we should have done the experiment outside. Oh well, I expect the carpet will dry off.

2. It's really hard to hit the fly, even when it's quite near and not moving. I wonder how the archer fish does it?

The science behind the experiment

1 Archer fish live in south-east Asia and parts of India and Australia. They mostly feed on small water insects but they can fire a 2-metre jet to bash bugs into the water.

2 The fast-firing fish uses its gills to pump water along a tube made by its tongue and the roof of its mouth. Baby archer fish aren't very good shots, but as they say, "practice makes perfect".

THAT'S MY THIRD TODAY!

WELL DONE, SIDNEY!

3 The experiment was inspired by reports in 2002 that archer fish in an aquarium in England were getting lazy on a diet of fish-food flakes. To train them up, staff smeared plastic flies with mushy meat and hung them above the fish tank. Direct hits knocked the free food down to the famished fish.

The Really Rotten Kids in… Copy cat

Animal-lover Chloë dreams of chatting in cat language…

MEOW! MEOW! *

PURR! PURR! **

HISS! HISS! ***

TRANSLATIONS: *GOOD MORNING, SLASHER!   **HELLO, CHLOË!   ***GET LOST!

Well, if that's your dream too you're in for a big surprise. Cats really can pass on messages! And if you know what they are, you can make contact with your cat. But have YOU got what it takes to talk to Tiddles?

HOW I MADE FRIENDS WITH A CAT
by Chloë

BEWARE OF DANGER!

Make friends with a cat you know — not a wild cat!

WHAT I NEEDED:
A cat (but not Slasher!)
A ball of string

WHAT I DID:

1. I chose a cat that I knew. I didn't try making friends with a strange cat because it might have been an escaped lion.

2. To start off with, I should have stuck my tail in the air — but I didn't have a tail. This is a friendly sign for a cat.

3. Instead I crouched down on my hands and knees and made short little meowing sounds.

ROLL!

THERE'S SOMETHING ODD ABOUT THAT CHILD

4. Then I rubbed faces with the cat.

5. I rolled on my back and waved my paws in the air. This means "come and play" in cat language.

6. But the cat just stared at me. So I got back on all fours and I wiggled my bottom. This is another "come and play" signal.

WHAT I FOUND:
When I got to stage 6, the cat decided to come and play. I waved the string and we chased it around the furniture. I made purring sounds to tell the cat I was happy. Then the string got tangled up in the furniture and Dad got tangled up in the string. Dad was cross, but I said I was doing my science homework and now he wants a word with Mr Bunsen...

The science behind the experiment

1 Of course, cats don't have a proper language like us humans, but they use actions to show what mood they're in.

2 They also use scent to send messages. Each cat has a special scent and if you want to make friends with a cat properly, you have to lick its face and sniff its bottom to sample its scent. But this is going a bit far even for *Really Rotten Experiments*…

3 Cats have a strict pecking order (or should that be PURRING order?), which lays down who's top cat. If two cats meet and can't agree who's boss, or if the cat meets another animal, it may try to act tough. But it's often a big fluffy bluff. Here's what happened when Slasher met Ripper…

SLASHER FLICKS HER TAIL TO BE FIERCE …
FLICK! FLICK!
WOOF!
BUT RIPPER THINKS SHE'S WAGGING HER TAIL TO BE FRIENDLY — JUST LIKE A DOG!

SLASHER FLUFFS HERSELF UP TO LOOK BIGGER AND GROWLS. THEN SHE STICKS OUT HER CLAWS AND HISSES.
HISS! STUPID CAT!

AND SO…
GROWL!
YIKES! HE'S BIGGER THAN ME!

The Really Rotten Kids in… Lounge lizard

It's incredible how a gecko can walk up walls and crawl across the ceiling. As Mr Bunsen is about to find out, these lizards really are champion climbers!

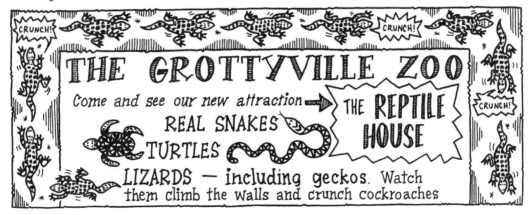

THE GROTTYVILLE ZOO
Come and see our new attraction → THE **REPTILE** HOUSE
REAL SNAKES
TURTLES
LIZARDS — including geckos. Watch them climb the walls and crunch cockroaches
CRUNCH!

THE KIDS ARE IN THE REPTILE HOUSE

CAN GECKOS CLIMB UP ANYTHING?

THEY CERTAINLY CAN!

GRRR — GET THIS THING OFF ME!

HOW I TESTED A GECKO
by Hannah

Here's one I made earlier

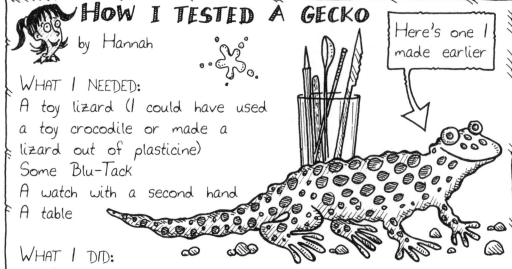

WHAT I NEEDED:
A toy lizard (I could have used a toy crocodile or made a lizard out of plasticine)
Some Blu-Tack
A watch with a second hand
A table

WHAT I DID:
1. I stuck the lizard to a wall using small pieces of Blu-Tack on the underside of its feet and timed how long it took to fall down.

2. Then I repeated the experiment, this time sticking the lizard to the underside of the table.

3. I repeated steps 1 and 2 using smaller lumps of Blu-Tack.

WHAT I FOUND:
1. The smaller the pieces of Blu-Tack I used, the quicker the lizard fell down. It also fell down faster when it was upside down.

2. The lizard did really well. It managed to cling to the underside of the table through supper. But then it fell on Auntie Beryl's foot. You should have heard her scream!

The science behind the experiment

1 A lizard will only stick to the ceiling if the sticking power in its feet is greater than the force of gravity trying to pull it down to the floor. Obviously geckos can do this, otherwise they'd be plopping into your tea every two minutes.

2 Geckos live in warm climates and spend their time munching insects. Although many types of gecko live in trees, they can make themselves at home in your home. And they can even hang by one toe from your ceiling.

3 In 2002, scientists found out how geckos can walk up walls and across the ceiling without falling. It's all thanks to microscopic hairs on their feet. The hairs enable them to grip anything – even polished glass.

The Really Rotten Kids in… Chimp champ

There's a new pupil at Rotten Road School. Chips the chimp has joined Mr Bunsen's class for an ape-intelligence experiment. But Chips is about to make a monkey of the other pupils…

The kids are annoyed with the ape. But then Chips disgraces himself by raiding Mr Bunsen's much-prized ant tank…

So Chips has to go… Oh well, at least the children have learnt an interesting lesson about how wild animals use tools to feed…

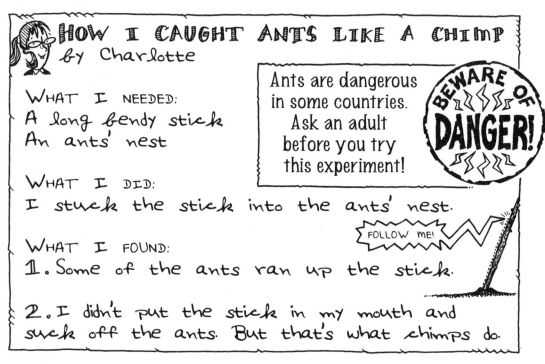

The science behind the experiment

1 Chimps swallow the insects fast before the ants nip their mouth and lips. This really is food with bite! The cunning chimps use stones to crack open nuts. And when chimps fancy a drink, they chew leaves and use them to soak up water. Then they squeeze the water out of the leaves and into their mouths. Can you be-leaf it?

2 Here are some other tools animals use…

• Smart sea otters use stones to crack open shellfish.
• Wise woodpecker finches from the Galapagos Islands use cactus spines to dig insects out of bark.
• Egg-headed Egyptian vultures drop stones on ostrich eggs to crack them open.
• On-the-ball orang-utans use large leaves as umbrellas.
• Educated elephants use sticks to scratch their big backs.
• Half-witted humans use tools for a strange ritual known as "DIY". But often their use of tools is primitive and clumsy.

3 All these creatures learn to use tools by copying a member of their family… And that reminds me – I wonder who taught Chips to catch Mr Bunsen's ants? Any ideas … *Charlotte*?

The Really Rotten Kids in… Skunk scamps

BUT LATER ...

WHAT MISS FITT DOESN'T SEE ...

HOW I DID THE SKUNK DANCE
by Rebecca

NICE PONG (READ NEXT PAGE TO FIND OUT WHAT SKUNK JUICE REALLY SMELLS LIKE!)

WHAT I NEEDED:
Some music with no singing in it (this wasn't vital), a clean, empty washing-up bottle, some water, a felt pen, a sticky label and some perfume

WHAT I DID:
1. I practised doing the skunk dance. Here's how Miss Fitt did it...

Stamp your feet and arch your back	Sway your body to and fro	Turn to your back and raise your tail...
	Walk towards your enemy...	

Give your enemy a good soaking!	Waggle your bum from side to side. 	READY ... STEADY ... FIRE!	Look over your shoulder and take aim... 

2. When I'd learnt the dance I half-filled the bottle with water, wrote "skunk juice" on the label and stuck it onto the side of the bottle.

3. I added ten squirts of perfume to give the skunk juice a scent.

4. When I did the dance I squirted water from the bottle and it looked like it came from my backside. It's a pity Mum got in the way!

WARNING!
Don't squirt your skunk juice in the house. And definitely don't try squirting skunk juice in posh restaurants!

The science behind the experiment

1 Skunks live in North America. If a skunk meets a larger creature, it dances the skunk dance to warn them off. But if that doesn't work, the skunk squirts stinky juice from juice-making glands in the base of its tail. It has a range of 5 metres.

2 Smelly skunk juice contains stinky substances called mercaptans – and they're said to be the WORST WHIFFS IN THE WHOLE WORLD. Just sniffing skunk juice can make you sick, and if it gets in your eyes, you won't be able to see for a while. The stink is so strong that you can sniff it 1.6 km away and it leaves your clothes honking for ONE WHOLE YEAR! Fancy a snort?

3 One traditional American treatment for a skunk stink is to take a bath in … tomato ketchup!

AT LEAST I'VE GOT SOMETHING TO DIP MY CHIPS IN!

The Really Rotten Kids in… I'll be dog-gone!

Your dog's sense of smell is better than your sense of smell – even if the dog doesn't smell as good as you! In fact, Sam's about to find out what super-sniffers dogs really are. You ought to know that he's hidden some unwanted school-dinner liver in his shoe…

But is your dog's sense of smell really that good? And how does your dog get the niffy news through his nose? I think I can feel an experiment coming on!

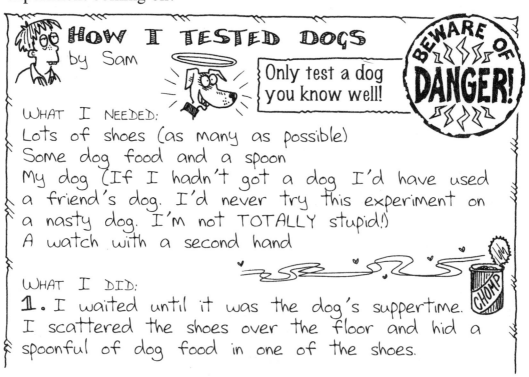

2. I let the dog into the room. (He wasn't allowed in while I was setting things up.) Then I watched and waited ... and timed how long it took the dog to find the food.

WHAT I FOUND:
1. I couldn't easily smell the dog food until I stuck my nose almost in the shoe. But the dog seemed to notice the smell as soon as he came into the room.

2. It wasn't long before he found the shoe with the dog food in it.

3. I forgot to clean the remains of the dog food out of the shoe and Dad got rather a nasty surprise when he put it on...

WHAT THE...?!

SPLURP!

Bet you never knew!
There are about 400 breeds of dog, but they're all the same type of animal and they're all descended from the wolf. And that means if you own a dog, there's a big, hairy, hungry, drooling wolf crouched in your living room. You'd better feed it before it starts to howl!

The science behind the experiment

1 Every animal is made of tiny microscopic living cells. Most cells have a special job to do in the body. A dog has many times more cells for detecting scent than you have.

2 The doggie's super sense of smell is handy for sniffing out food. And, like many other animals, dogs use scent to pass on messages. That's why dogs sniff and pee on lampposts. The stinky smell tells other dogs they passed that way. So the lamppost is a sort of doggy message board.

3 Scientists reckon that a bloodhound's sense of smell is ONE MILLION times better than your sense of smell. These super-sensitive sniffers can tell the difference between your scent and that of your brother or sister. In fact their super-charged schnozzles prefer sniffing out smells a few days old because fresh smells are way too whiffy! I guess stinky school dinners would be deadly!

Queasy quiz 3

Hopefully you're amused and amazed by the animal antics of the furry friends in this chapter. And that means you'll be straining at the leash to answer a few curious creature-feature quiz questions!

In this quiz, made-up newspaper headlines are used to report real experiments, but the words LITTLE BROTHER have been used to hide the names of the animals involved. Your job is to work out which animal belongs to which experiment...

Headlines:

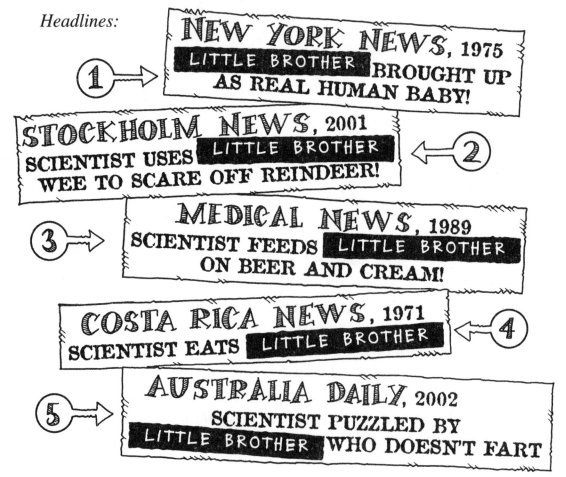

1 → NEW YORK NEWS, 1975
LITTLE BROTHER BROUGHT UP AS REAL HUMAN BABY!

STOCKHOLM NEWS, 2001
SCIENTIST USES LITTLE BROTHER WEE TO SCARE OFF REINDEER! ← 2

3 → MEDICAL NEWS, 1989
SCIENTIST FEEDS LITTLE BROTHER ON BEER AND CREAM!

COSTA RICA NEWS, 1971
SCIENTIST EATS LITTLE BROTHER ← 4

5 → AUSTRALIA DAILY, 2002
SCIENTIST PUZZLED BY LITTLE BROTHER WHO DOESN'T FART

Animals:
a) *Kangaroo* **b)** *Wolf* **c)** *Chimp*

d) *Tadpole* **e)** *Leech*

Answers:

1 c) A baby chimp named Nim was taught sign language for the deaf. Nim learnt fewer signs than a human baby would, but proved far more naughty. He often trashed the houses he lived in. Now you might think Nim sounds a bit like your baby brother, but at least your baby brother doesn't swing from the light fittings and chuck bananas at you … or does he?

2 b) Wolf pee was supposed to stop the reindeer wandering on to railway tracks with messy results for the reindeer. It didn't work, so the bosses of Sweden's railways tried playing radio music and chat through loudspeakers. I wonder if they played reindeer requests?

3 e) Bloodsucking leeches help surgeons by keeping blood flowing through damaged blood vessels while the surgeon sews a chopped-off finger back on to its rightful owner. But what happens if the leeches aren't peckish? Well, traditionally surgeons used cream to get the lazy leeches lunching again and beer was said to make listless leeches lively… But then fearless Norwegian scientists Anders Baerheim and Hogne Sandvik fed these foods to leeches before letting them suck Sandvik's blood. And they found that…

WAS IT CLOTTED CREAM?

NO, IT WAS CLOTTED BLOOD… I HAD TO DRINK FOUR PINTS OF BEER TO GET RID OF THE TASTE!

• Leeches who drank beer got drunk (shurely shum mishtake here!)

• And drinking cream didn't make leeches feed more than usual.

So now you know – leeches fear beer and scream at cream!

4 d) In 1971, scientist Richard Wasserug talked a group of science students into tucking into tadpoles to discover how they tasted. He wanted to know if certain tadpoles were brightly coloured to warn larger animals that they tasted vile. (That is, even more vile than any other tadpoles.) For the experiment, they had to put a slimy tadpole in their mouths and chew it for 40 seconds before spitting it out. Now you might think this sounds cruel to tadpoles (and science students). But for many years, suffering school children were forced to eat frogspawn (also known as sago pudding). And they weren't even allowed to spit it out!

5 a) In 2002, scientists in Queensland, Australia, tried to find out why kangaroos don't fart as much as sheep and cows. They were looking for germs in kangaroo guts that stop the animals bottom-burping methane gas – or to put it another way…

BRAINY BOFFINS BET ON BOUNCING BOUNDER'S BOTTOM BACTERIA BREAKTHROUGH!

How's that for a hard-hitting headline?

Mind you, talking about smelly gas brings us on to the madly mixed-up subject of chemistry. And by a really rotten coincidence, chemistry is the smelly subject of our next crazy chapter…

Crazy chemistry experiments

We live in a world of mixed-up chemicals and we're made of mixed-up chemicals too. And if that sounds confusing, you really need to read this chapter and get your hands messy with some seriously soggy and smelly substance experiments…

By mixing up a few chemicals you might become less mixed-up about chemistry.

The Really Rotten Kids in… Slime time

What's the difference between slime and school-dinner custard?

Well, *you* might think they're the same – but any chemist will tell you there's a big difference. There's the colour, for one thing … and the taste. The taste of slime will stay with you for a very long time. As Mr Bunsen is about to find out…

If you've ever thought about making your own evil-looking slime, you've come to the right place. Just don't try feeding it to your teacher!

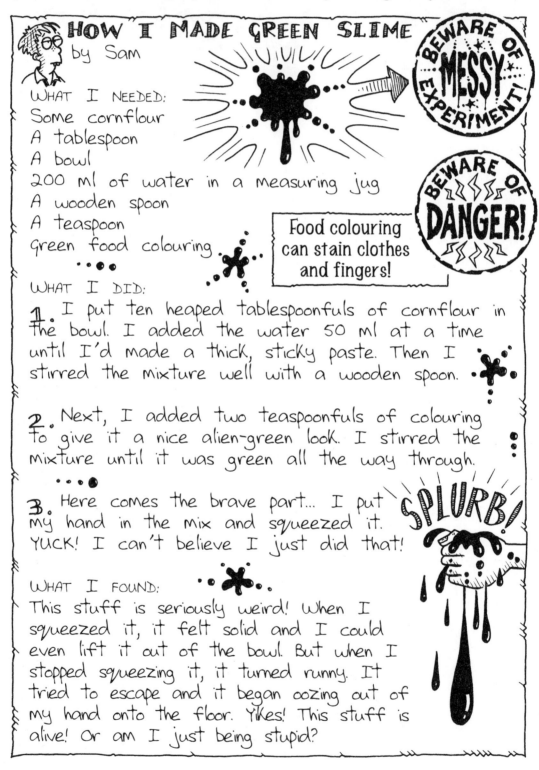

HOW I MADE GREEN SLIME
by Sam

BEWARE OF MESSY EXPERIMENT!

BEWARE OF DANGER!

WHAT I NEEDED:
Some cornflour
A tablespoon
A bowl
200 ml of water in a measuring jug
A wooden spoon
A teaspoon
Green food colouring

Food colouring can stain clothes and fingers!

WHAT I DID:

1. I put ten heaped tablespoonfuls of cornflour in the bowl. I added the water 50 ml at a time until I'd made a thick, sticky paste. Then I stirred the mixture well with a wooden spoon.

2. Next, I added two teaspoonfuls of colouring to give it a nice alien-green look. I stirred the mixture until it was green all the way through.

3. Here comes the brave part... I put my hand in the mix and squeezed it. YUCK! I can't believe I just did that!

SPLURB!

WHAT I FOUND:
This stuff is seriously weird! When I squeezed it, it felt solid and I could even lift it out of the bowl. But when I stopped squeezing it, it turned runny. It tried to escape and it began oozing out of my hand onto the floor. Yikes! This stuff is alive! Or am I just being stupid?

The science behind the experiment

1 No, the slime *wasn't* alive, worst luck! It's all to do with the substances that it contains.

2 Water is made up of tiny objects called molecules (moll-eck-ules).

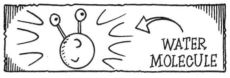

This is nothing to do with a small, blind underground creature with an ice lolly.

3 Now imagine you were shrunk down to the size of a molecule. You'd see grains of cornflour as giant cages made of molecules. And when the water gets mixed with the cornflour, the much larger cornflour grains float about in a sea of water molecules.

4 But when you squeeze the mix, the water molecules get squashed inside the grains.

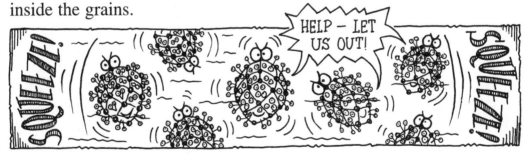

This makes the green slime less runny.

5 When you relax your grip, out pop the water molecules again!

The Really Rotten Kids in… Ice ain't nice

Mr Bunsen decides that a freezing day is a good time for a lesson about cold. But he gets a frosty reception from the kids…

WHAT I DID:

1. I drew the outline of a person on the leaf. It looked a bit like Mr Bunsen.

2. I cut out the figure and drew Mr Bunsen's face and Mr Bunsen's clothes on it, and it looked just like my teacher. Then I dunked Mr Bunsen into the bowl of water.

3. I put the bowl in the freezer. After a couple of hours I rescued Mr Bunsen and left him to thaw out.

WHAT I FOUND:

When I took Mr Bunsen out of the freezer, he was frozen solid in the ice. After he had thawed out, Mr Bunsen looked saggier and darker than he'd been before. To check this I compared Mr Bunsen with the rest of the leaf. I was right, Mr Bunsen was in a bad way!

The science behind the experiment

1 Once again, Mr B's got the ball rolling with the nitty-gritty science stuff. Cold is indeed lack of heat energy…

2 Molecules are always moving and fidgeting about, a bit like the Rotten Road kids. But cold molecules have less energy and move more slowly. And that means they don't bounce apart even when they bump into each other. Water molecules can stick together to form solid structures called crystals. And ice is a mass of water crystals.

3 Ice can be nice...

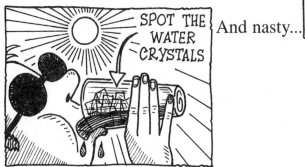

And nasty...

4 Although the body is about 60 per cent water, it's horribly hard to freeze a human body. The body stores warmth and much of the water is mingled with other substances that don't freeze as easily.

5 When a body does freeze, ice crystals rip open the cells that make it up. This is what happened to the leaf figure too – the ice crystals smashed open the cells like a hungry bear in a honey store. When the human body thaws out, it's all soggy and squishy like the leaf. OH, YUCK!

6 With its cells ripped open, the thawed-out leaf was mushy and weakened inside and this made it soggy. The green substance in the leaf – known as chlorophyll (klor-o-fill) – had been damaged and this gave the leaf a darker colour.

The Really Rotten Kids in…Weird water

Water is amazing stuff – it's even got a "skin". But why? Mr Bunsen is about to get rather wet finding out…

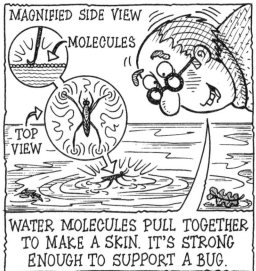

70

BUT MR B LEANS TOO FAR...

SPLOSH!

GLUG!

BUT NOT STRONG ENOUGH TO SUPPORT MR B!

EEK!

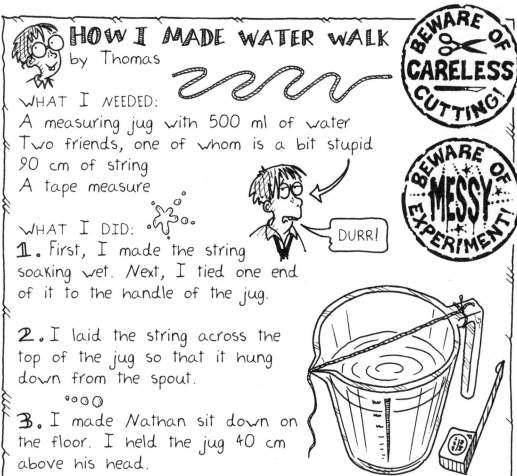

HOW I MADE WATER WALK
by Thomas

WHAT I NEEDED:
A measuring jug with 500 ml of water
Two friends, one of whom is a bit stupid
90 cm of string
A tape measure

DURR!

WHAT I DID:
1. First, I made the string soaking wet. Next, I tied one end of it to the handle of the jug.

2. I laid the string across the top of the jug so that it hung down from the spout.

3. I made Nathan sit down on the floor. I held the jug 40 cm above his head.

BEWARE OF CARELESS CUTTING!

BEWARE OF MESSY EXPERIMENT!

4. Sam had to sit down on the floor and hold the end of the string tightly on his head. He was sitting next to Nathan with just enough space between them to make the string tight.

5. I tipped the jug gently so that the water started to spill out of the spout...

GRINNING IDIOT

90 CM

TIP!

40 CM

WORRIED SWOT

WHAT I FOUND:

1. The string had to be tight and touching the spout. Most of the water ran down the string and onto Sam's head!

2. I tried to hold the jug steady, but a bit of water dripped on Nathan's head.

3. My friends made me hold the string. And that's when I got wet!

DRIP!

The science behind the experiment

1 The water ran down the string because gravity pulled it down. But surface tension kept the drops of water together in a stream.
2 This is how surface tension works. Each molecule of water is made up of three atoms … two hydrogen and one oxygen. Here's a close-up view of what they look like:

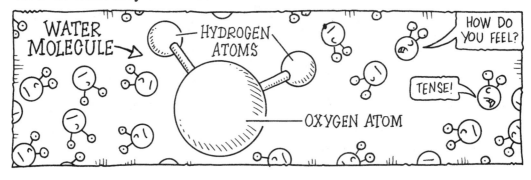

WATER MOLECULE → HYDROGEN ATOMS

HOW DO YOU FEEL?

TENSE!

OXYGEN ATOM

While the oxygen atom happily hangs on to the hydrogen atoms, it also tugs at hydrogen atoms from other water molecules. This pulls the water drops together. It also helps to make ice (see page 69).

3 Surface tension is stronger than gravity – and that's why the water doesn't plip and plop on Nathan's head.

The Really Rotten Kids in… Soak it and see

Some science is like magic…

If you tried this, I bet you'd want to show everyone. But remember, you've got to set up the experiment right. Otherwise it's a washout… Look what happened when Mr Bunsen tried the experiment in class!

So why didn't the water fall out of the glass the first time? Well, as you've probably guessed, the secret's in the science. And you can find out the science secret by trying the experiment for yourself!

HOW I STOPPED WATER FLOWING
by Hannah

WHAT I NEEDED:
A tall glass
Some water
A tea towel or a scrap of tea towel large enough to cover the top of the glass. I couldn't find a tea towel so I used my dad's underpants.
A strong elastic band
A friend

WHAT I DID:
1. I filled the glass with water.

2. Next, I placed the underpants over the glass. I wrapped the elastic band twice around the underpants and the glass to keep them in place.

3. I made Katie sit on the floor.

4. I turned the glass upside down. Katie screamed but...

WHAT I FOUND:
No water came out! My dad was a bit upset about his soggy underpants, though....

GRRRRR!

The science behind the experiment

1 Remember surface tension? Remember how it's all thanks to those ever-so-friendly water molecules that just want to stick together? Well, here they're up to their old tricks again…

2 The water molecules get together to make surface tension across the holes of the cloth. Imagine about five children holding hands trying to go through a door all at once. They won't fit through and it's just the same for the water molecules and the holes. As long as they stick together, none of them can slip through. So Katie stays dry!

Bet you never knew!

A drop of water contains about 1,700 billion molecules. That means that on a hot day, you sweat squillions of molecules. But don't worry – you won't dry out. Your body contains over 20 litres of the wet drippy stuff.

The Really Rotten Kids in… Fizzy fun!

Shake a can of fizzy drink a few times, then open it up. What d'ya think happens next? Hey *don't* try it! Let's see what happens to Mr Bunsen…

But what's going on inside the can to make the fizz fly? And is there any way to stop it? We'll need an experiment to find that out. But first here's a fascinating frothy fact…

Bet you never knew!

A fizzy drink gets its fizz from carbon-dioxide gas. The carbon dioxide gets forced into the drink until the gas dissolves. Often the gas is made by microbes called yeasts that feed on sugar. And that means your lovely bubbly fizzy drink is bubbling with mouldy microbe burps. Don't get hiccups now!

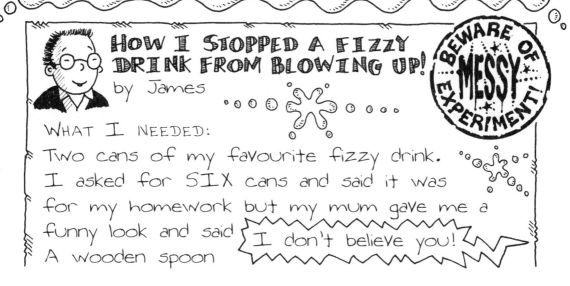

HOW I STOPPED A FIZZY DRINK FROM BLOWING UP!
by James

BEWARE OF MESSY EXPERIMENT!

WHAT I NEEDED:
Two cans of my favourite fizzy drink. I asked for SIX cans and said it was for my homework but my mum gave me a funny look and said I don't believe you!
A wooden spoon

WHAT I DID:
1. I shook up the first can five times and opened the top. The drink sprayed everywhere and loads of bubbles came out. The drink made a sticky mess and Mum told me off. It was then that I realized that I should have done the experiment outside.

2. I drank what was left of the first drink and went outside and shook the second can five times. But this time I gently tapped the top of the can with the side of the spoon ten times. I began to open the can ... the dog dived for cover, my little brother hid in the shed and...

WHAT I FOUND:
Nothing happened! The drink frothed a bit but none of it got spilt. Until I poured it into my mouth and some of it went down my shirt...

The science behind the experiment

1 When you shake the drink, you mix up the air in the top of the can with the drink to make air bubbles…

The carbon-dioxide gas moves into the air bubbles.
2 Inside the bubble the carbon-dioxide molecules can spread out. This makes the bubbles bigger.

3 If you open the shaken can, the bubbles explode from the drink and you get sticky.

4 When you tap the can a few times, you burst the bubbles. The gas goes back to being dissolved and you can enjoy a nice, peaceful drink.

Well, fairly peaceful!

Queasy quiz 4

And now, if you're not still burping with too much gas, choc-a-bloc with too many solids and awash with too many liquids, here's the fearsome fourth in our queasy quiz series. Can you crack the chemistry code?

INSTRUCTIONS

First, answer the questions – there are clues to help you! Then put the first letter of each answer together to spell a type of chemical mentioned in the chapter. Got all that?

1 A substance found in the sweat from these body parts has been used in a perfume – what is the body part? Clue: These two places are the PITS!

2 Which substance did Swiss scientists try to melt using a laser beam in 1995? Clue: In Switzerland this substance is sometimes full of holes.

3 What substance did US magician David Blaine live inside in 2000? Clue: You might find it in drinks but it's not runny!

4 Scientist Len Fisher wanted to find out the ideal state of sogginess of a gingernut biscuit. So he made a cup of tea. What did he do with the biscuit?
Clue: Think of a word that rhymes with "junk".
5 In 2001, Buck Weimer of Colorado, USA, invented a new kind of underwear. What, according to Buck, did his underwear NOT do?
Clue: What do noses do?

Answers:

1 ARMPITS. The perfume, Andron, contained a substance that gives armpit sweat a musky smell. You may like to know that among the other substances found in armpit sweat is one that pongs like stale pee. And there's another that stinks like a smelly male goat and makes female goats a bit frisky.

2 CHEESE. The scientists made a Swiss dish called raclette, in which the cheese is melted in stages as you eat it. The experiment wasn't too serious but the results were seriously tasty.

3 ICE. He lived inside a block of ice for 58 hours – that's two and a half days. The magician was getting air and water through a tube, so he was in little danger. Air spaces trapped in the ice stop heat from escaping quickly, just like a duvet. The inside of the ice block was as warm and cosy as an igloo, and that's not as bad as you think…

4 DUNK IT. The scientist dunked the biscuit into the tea and found that the ideal dunking time is based on the size of the tiny holes in the biscuit. For a gingernut it's three seconds but for a digestive biscuit it's a full eight seconds. So now you know. By the way, some teachers I know violently disagree with this result, so you might like to try your own experiments…

5 SMELL.

Did you work out the hidden word? It's ACIDS.

Now, purely in the interests of entertainment, here's some more about Buck Weimer and his incredible underwear, with their motto – "Wear them for the one you love". I bet you've been waiting all your life to own a pair. Or even better, the chance to make your little brother, dog or granny *wear* a pair…

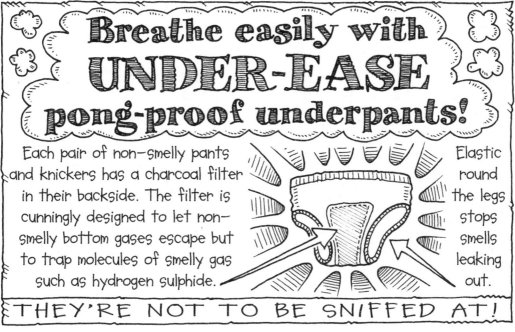

I'm pleased to say that Buck Weimer won an Ig Nobel Prize for his incredible invention. These much-coveted awards are presented at Harvard University, USA. They're awarded for off-beat science, and several experiments in this book have received them. In accepting the award, Buck waved a pair of pants at the audience and sang a song.

And I'm sure you'll agree that's a beautiful thought to take with us into our next stomach-churning chapter on foul physics…

Foul physics experiments

Physics can make you physic-ally sick. It's the sickening science of forces and energy and electricity and magnetism and light and sound and heat and, well, I could go on and on. But if I did, it would take you 20 years to read this book and you'd need a dumper truck to take it home from the bookshop. So I'll sum up physics by saying it's about everything that makes the universe tick. And that's more than enough – as you'll be finding out…

The Really Rotten Kids in… Egg-speriment

What's in an egg? Well, it's a sort of spacecraft for baby chickens to live and grow in until they're ready to hatch. And it comes complete with a gloopy yolk and white for the chick to feed on. But the egg also has a tremendous science secret. It can withstand amazing weights – as Mr Bunsen is about to show us…

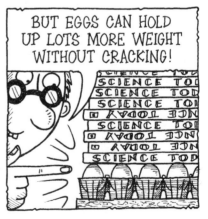

While Mr Bunsen is making a hasty *eggs-it*, I've just got time to say that the next experiment will show you what makes eggs so strong… Over to you, Sam!

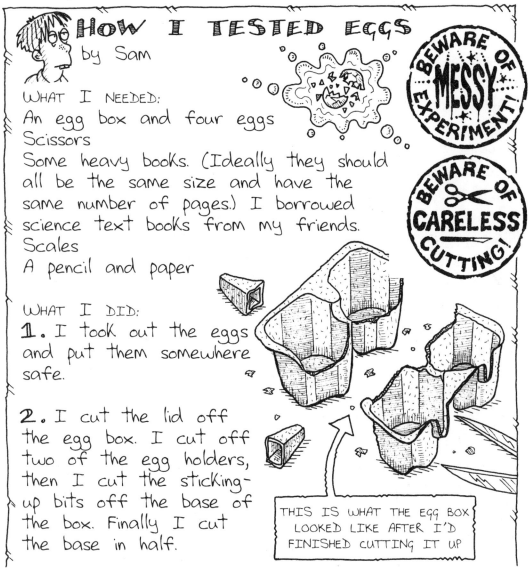

HOW I TESTED EGGS
by Sam

BEWARE OF MESSY EXPERIMENT!

BEWARE OF CARELESS CUTTING!

WHAT I NEEDED:
An egg box and four eggs
Scissors
Some heavy books. (Ideally they should all be the same size and have the same number of pages.) I borrowed science text books from my friends.
Scales
A pencil and paper

WHAT I DID:
1. I took out the eggs and put them somewhere safe.

2. I cut the lid off the egg box. I cut off two of the egg holders, then I cut the sticking-up bits off the base of the box. Finally I cut the base in half.

THIS IS WHAT THE EGG BOX LOOKED LIKE AFTER I'D FINISHED CUTTING IT UP

81

3. I put the eggs in each half of the base with the small ends pointing up. I laid the two halves on a table.

4. Next, I weighed one of the books and noted the weight. I laid the book on top of the eggs.

5. I piled books on top of each other until the eggs cracked.

WHAT I FOUND:

1. The eggs held up all the heavy science text books and I had to borrow some more from Nathan.

2. When the eggs broke, the yolks went all over the books. But it was OK because the text books were pretty messy already.

The science behind the experiment

1 An egg is surprisingly strong – it has to be, to protect the cute little baby chick growing inside it.

2 The ends of an egg are rounded. When you put a book on top of an egg, the curved top takes the force and spreads it around the egg's sides. There's less force pressing on the top of the egg – so the egg can take a weight of 22.7 kg without cracking…

3 If eggs had flat tops, they'd be far weaker. Take a look at this…

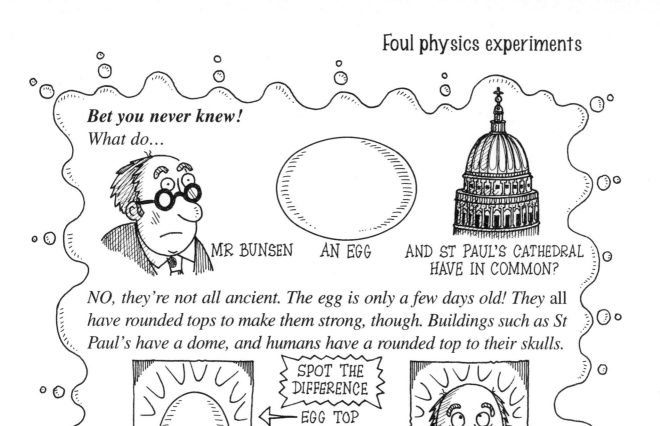

Bet you never knew!
What do…

MR BUNSEN   AN EGG   AND ST PAUL'S CATHEDRAL HAVE IN COMMON?

NO, they're not all ancient. The egg is only a few days old! They all have rounded tops to make them strong, though. Buildings such as St Paul's have a dome, and humans have a rounded top to their skulls.

SPOT THE DIFFERENCE

EGG TOP

EGG-HEAD TEACHER

The Really Rotten Kids in… Banger clanger

When Mr Bunsen tries to teach his class about the science of sound, he has to give them an ear-bashing to get a fair hearing…

THIS LESSON IS ABOUT SOUND…

CHATTER!

WILL YOU BE QUIET?!

SILENCE!

BUT SOON…

SOUND IS MADE UP OF SOUND WAVES THAT TRAVEL THROUGH THE AIR…

CHATTER! CHATTER!

CLANG! CLANG! CLANG!

DAZED SILENCE!

BUT THE KIDS ARE STILL CHATTING…

THIS WILL SHUT THEM UP!

DUH! DUH! DUH!

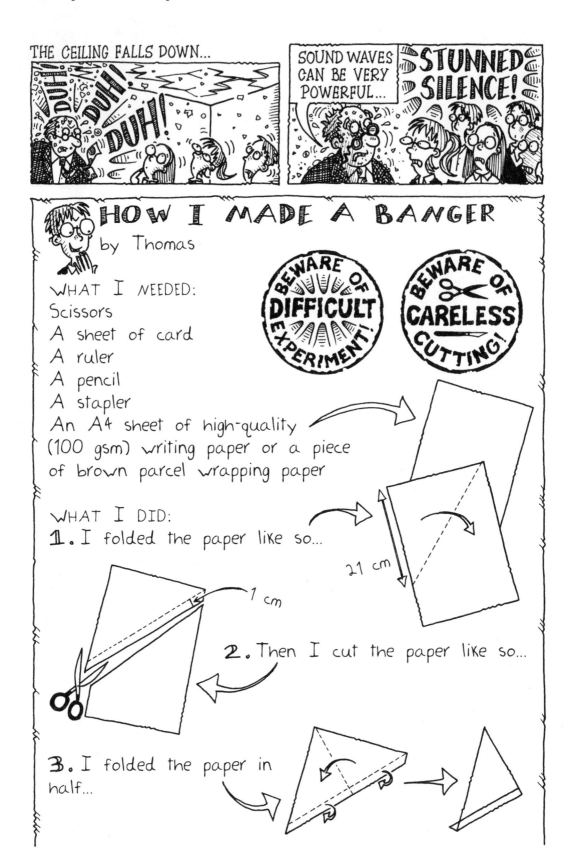

THE CEILING FALLS DOWN... DUH! DUH! DUH!

SOUND WAVES CAN BE VERY POWERFUL... STUNNED SILENCE!

HOW I MADE A BANGER
by Thomas

BEWARE OF DIFFICULT EXPERIMENT!

BEWARE OF CARELESS CUTTING!

WHAT I NEEDED:
Scissors
A sheet of card
A ruler
A pencil
A stapler
An A4 sheet of high-quality (100 gsm) writing paper or a piece of brown parcel wrapping paper

WHAT I DID:

1. I folded the paper like so...

21 cm

1 cm

2. Then I cut the paper like so...

3. I folded the paper in half...

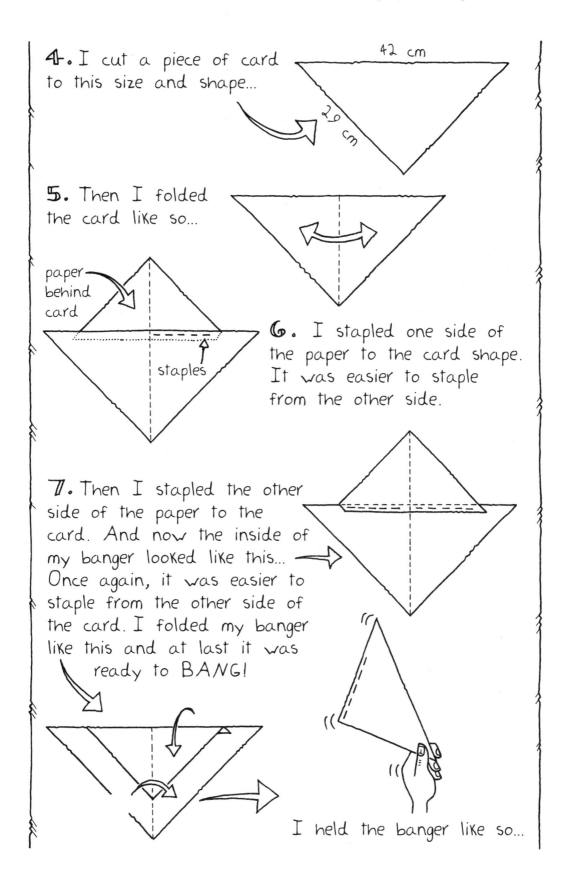

4. I cut a piece of card to this size and shape...

42 cm

29 cm

5. Then I folded the card like so...

paper behind card

staples

6. I stapled one side of the paper to the card shape. It was easier to staple from the other side.

7. Then I stapled the other side of the paper to the card. And now the inside of my banger looked like this... Once again, it was easier to staple from the other side of the card. I folded my banger like this and at last it was ready to BANG!

I held the banger like so...

85

8. And whacked it down as fast as I could.

BANG!

WHAT I FOUND:
It made a brilliant bang! My little sister jumped a metre in the air, my mum dropped the teapot and the budgie fell off his perch. I got my pocket money stopped to pay for the teapot. But I told mum the banger was my science homework and then Mr Bunsen got the blame.

GRRR – I'LL HAVE A WORD WITH THAT MR BUNSEN!

The science behind the experiment

1 When you whack the banger down, the folded paper traps air so fast that it can't escape. The air pushes back on the paper, unfolding it so fast that it releases some of its energy as sound waves.

2 A sound wave zooms through the air and sets the air molecules moving. It's like a ripple on a pond.

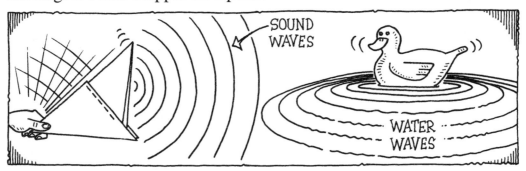

SOUND WAVES

WATER WAVES

3 Your ears are designed to pick up sound waves and your brain makes sense of the pattern they make. Well, sometimes…

The Really Rotten Kids in… Funny money

Matt always seems to have masses of money. But what's the secret of having lashings of lolly? Well, it turns out that Matt knows a sly scientific scam to do with air. The trick is guaranteed to work on gullible parents … and teachers.

Once you know the secret, you might like to try it yourself … at your own risk, of course!

WHAT I DID:
1. I bet Mr Bunsen £5 that I could put a banknote underwater without it getting wet.

2. I screwed up the banknote and stuck it inside the glass at the bottom. I used Blu-Tack to hold the banknote in place.

3. Then I turned the glass upside down and pushed it under the water.

WHAT I FOUND:
The banknote stayed dry and I got £5 richer – ha ha!

The science behind the experiment

1 Air takes up a certain amount of space and it actually pushes against you. This force is called "air pressure".

2 You probably don't feel too squashed by air pressure, but that's because you've been feeling it squishing down on your body ever since you were born. You're so used to it that you don't notice it.

3 Air pressure inside the glass is strong enough to keep the water out.

Bet you never knew!

Air pressure is horribly vital. If you went into space without a spacesuit, there'd be no air pressure pressing on your body. But there would be air pressure from the air inside your lungs and guts. With no air pressure on the outside to balance the pressure inside your body, your lungs and guts would explode with horribly messy results.

The Really Rotten Kids in… Puff pant!

Air pressure is essential for a bicycle to work, as Mr Bunsen is about to explain. And terrible Thomas uses air pressure to play a perilous practical joke.

Hmm – it looks like Mr Bunsen *tyres* easily, ha ha! And now here's Thomas to show how air pressure helps you to suck drink through a straw and play tricks on your friends…

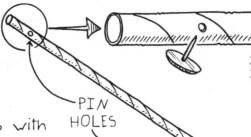

WHAT I DID:

1. Using the drawing pin, I made a hole at each end of the drinking straw.

PIN HOLES

2. I filled one of the bottles with water and stuck the straw in it.

3. Using the drawing pin, I punched ten holes in the bottom of the other bottle. I filled the bottle with water from the tap and the water dripped through the holes. No surprises so far...

4. When the bottle was full of water, I put on the top.

5. I invited James and Matt round for a nice cold drink.

WHAT I FOUND:

1. Matt sucked and sucked on the straw but he couldn't suck any drink from his bottle.

2. The bottle with the holes in didn't leak ... until James took the top off. Then it leaked a lot and James got water all down his trousers.

3. Matt and James chased me. When they caught me, they poured the rest of their drinks over my head.

The science behind the experiment

1 Both the trick straw and the trick bottle work because of air pressure...

2 When you suck through a straw, first you suck the air from the straw into your mouth. The air pressure pushes down on the drink and pushes the drink up the straw and into your thirsty throat. In other words, air pressure does the hard work...

SLURP!

AIR PRESSURE

But the holes in the straw mess things up. As fast as you suck air up the straw, more air pours into the straw. As long as there's air in the straw, the air pressure can't drop and that means the air pressure on the drink can't push it up the straw.

3 Still with me? Great – now for the bottle. Let's take a look at the fascinating forces at work…

As you found out on page 72, surface tension gives water a stretchy skin and it doesn't like being forced through holes.

4 But when you take the top off the bottle, the outside air pressure crashes down into the bottle. The awesome air pressure is strong enough to push the water through the holes. And then your socks get a soaking…

AIR PRESSURE BLOCKED BY TOP

AIR TRAPPED IN BOTTLE DOESN'T HAVE ENOUGH PRESSURE TO PUSH WATER OUT

Bet you never knew!

The longest straw you could drink through is about 10 metres long. You can't suck through a longer straw because air pressure is only strong enough to push water to this height. And even a thirsty elephant couldn't suck its drink through a longer straw.

The Really Rotten Kids in… Flour power

WOW! COOL! THAT WAS SOME EXPLOSION!

BOOM!

OH RATS! We've missed a really incredible experiment. Mr Bunsen was showing the kids how air pressure turns flour into a volcano.

Never mind, you can always try the experiment yourself. Just make sure you try it outside – on pain of DEATH!

Bet you never knew!

Real volcanoes can explode because of gas pressure. Super-heated gas builds up inside the volcano. The gas can't escape because rocks block the opening of the volcano. At last the pressure gets strong enough to blast the rocks out of the way and then … KA-BOOOM!

HOW I MADE A FLOUR VOLCANO
by Matt

BEWARE OF MESSY EXPERIMENT!

WHAT I NEEDED:
A balloon
A funnel
A friend
A tablespoon
Some flour

WHAT I DID:

1. I did the experiment in the garden. Mum said if I dared do it in the house, I'd have to advertise in the paper for new parents. Now that gives me an idea!

2. I blew up the balloon a few times to make it baggy.

3. Then I blew up the balloon and twisted its neck.

4. While I pinched the twisted neck of the balloon tightly to stop the air getting out, my friend Thomas pulled the opening of the balloon over the neck of the funnel.

5. Thomas put four tablespoonfuls of flour into the funnel. My burster was ready for the BIG BLOW-UP!

FUNNEL

NECK OF BALLOON

TWISTED BIT

BALLOON

WHAT I FOUND:
I held the funnel up in the air and let the balloon neck untwist. WOW! The flour blew up like a volcano! I didn't expect the cat to walk past, did I? Oh well, at least she's all white ... er, I mean all right.

The science behind the experiment

1 When you blow up a balloon, you're puffing air into it (howls of amazement here).

2 As you blow air into the balloon, the air pressure builds up. Soon it's stronger than the air pressure squishing on the balloon from outside.

3 The air pressure inside the balloon is strong enough to push the sides of the balloon outwards. It's just like Mr B's tyres on page 89!

4 But the stretchy rubber sides of the balloon are pushing back and trying to get the air out of the balloon. And the air pressing outside is still pressing in.

5 When you let go of the neck of the balloon, these forces blast the air out of the balloon. And the air fires the flour like a volcano.

The Really Rotten Kids in… Krazy krispies

Here's something new at Rotten Road School…

JOIN THE ROTTEN ROAD SCHOOL BREAKFAST CLUB

ENJOY BREAKFAST WITH YOUR FRIENDS

AND CATCH UP ON YOUR HOMEWORK!

But what's turned Mr Bunsen's breakfast into a battle? Well, it's all due to a fearsome force and you can get to grips with it in the next hair-raising experiment…

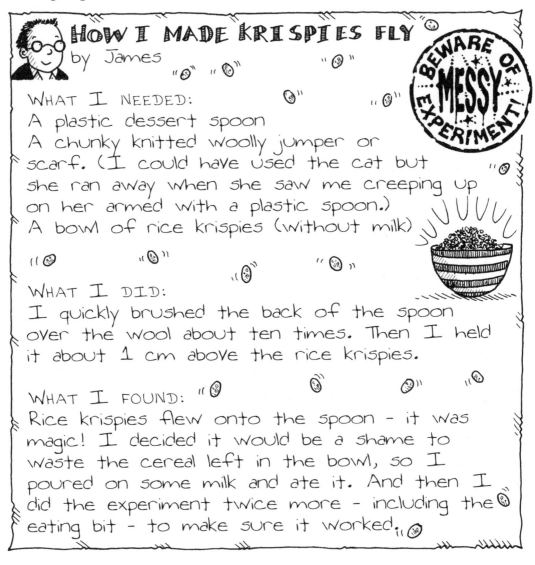

HOW I MADE KRISPIES FLY
by James

WHAT I NEEDED:
A plastic dessert spoon
A chunky knitted woolly jumper or scarf. (I could have used the cat but she ran away when she saw me creeping up on her armed with a plastic spoon.)
A bowl of rice krispies (without milk)

WHAT I DID:
I quickly brushed the back of the spoon over the wool about ten times. Then I held it about 1 cm above the rice krispies.

WHAT I FOUND:
Rice krispies flew onto the spoon – it was magic! I decided it would be a shame to waste the cereal left in the bowl, so I poured on some milk and ate it. And then I did the experiment twice more – including the eating bit – to make sure it worked.

The science behind the experiment

1 To make sense of the experiment, you need to take a very close look at this atom.

2 The electrons and nucleus pull on each other and this holds the atom together. And if you want to sound like a scientist, you can call the pulling force by its name – the electromagnetic (e-leck-tro-mag-ne-tick) force.

3 And now for Mr Bunsen's flying krispies. When Mr B rubbed his spoon on his trousers, he rubbed billions of electrons off the material. The electrons pulled on the atoms of the krispies. And those teeny-tiny electrons had enough power to tug the krispies into the air. This electrifying effect is called "static electricity".

4 You can use the spoon to make the cat's fur, or even your hair, stand up for the same reason.

Queasy quiz 5

Let's hope you're not fully fed up with physics because it's time for another quirky quiz and, as luck would have it, it's on physics! Can you work out the result of these strange scientific studies?

A note from the author – these rotten researches really happened – honest!

1 I studied the effects of being hit by a falling coconut.

Possible results …
a) The scientist was knocked out by a coconut.
b) The scientist discovered that a falling coconut can be deadly.
c) The scientist found out that being hit by a falling coconut can give you a nasty headache.

2 We created a magnetic frog.

Possible results…
a) The frog glowed in the dark.
b) The frog floated in mid-air.
c) The frog stuck to the scientist's fridge and it needed six strong men to pull it off.

3 We wanted to know why toilets collapse and cause the sort of injuries that you don't really want to imagine.

Possible results…
a) The toilets collapse because heavy people sit on them.
b) The toilets collapse because some people like to bounce up and down on the toilet seat.
c) The toilets collapse because they're worn out.

4 We built a kangaroo crash-test dummy.

Possible results…
a) The kangaroo dummy hopped clear of the crashing car.
b) The kangaroo dummy got bashed just as it was designed to do.
c) The car got wrecked but the kangaroo dummy happily hopped away without a scratch.

5 We measured the sound of a champion burper's burp.

Possible results…
a) The burp was so loud that it broke the sound-measuring machine.
b) The burp was as loud as a plane taking off.
c) A nearby child burped even louder than the burping champion.

Answers:

1 b) And now for the coco-nutty details in a nutshell. Canadian doctor Peter Barss studied injuries caused by falling coconuts in Papua New Guinea. It's a great example of gravity in action and how strong the round-topped human head is. Peter found that a falling coconut can reach a speed of 80 km an hour. Most coconut injuries aren't fatal, but getting nutted on the nut by a falling nut sometimes is.

2 b) Yes – we live in the age of the flying frog. All credit to Andre Geim and Sir Michael Berry for using a super-strong magnet to magnetize a frog and lift it into the air. The scientists also made strawberries and nuts fly. If they had a strong enough magnet, you too could hover without bovver.

3 c) The Scottish scientists who bravely looked into the question thought it might be because the toilets were old and worn out. I guess ancient toilets are a bit like elderly teachers – they have to be treated with respect or they might do you an injury. Or to put it another way: look after your bott and be careful when you squat!

4 b) In 2000, an Australian car-maker proudly unveiled the world's first kangaroo crash-test dummy. (In Australia, thousands of 'roos hop in front of speeding cars with rotten results for the 'roos.)

5 b) The burp was made at the Science Museum in London, in 2002, by burping champion Paul Hunn. Sadly all the hype was a lot of hot air. It was all sound and fury as Paul failed to improve on his best-ever world-record burp. Well, pardon me!

Fearsome finale

Welcome to the end of this book! We're here at Rotten Road School to award the Horrible Science Really Rotten Experiments Awards for the most horrible experiments ever…

The Third Prize goes to…

The University of Toronto in Canada and their incredible spinning bed in a spinning room. You lie on it to experience the effects of being space sick. A TV presenter who bravely tried the test called it…

> The most hideous sensation your body can give you. This is really, really nasty!

The Second Prize goes to…

The Scottish doctor who tested how people stand up to physical exhaustion…

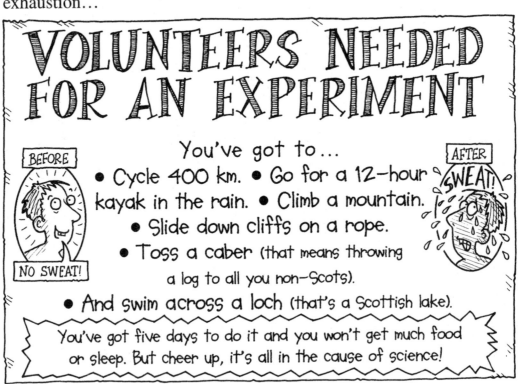

VOLUNTEERS NEEDED FOR AN EXPERIMENT

BEFORE
NO SWEAT!

AFTER
SWEAT!

You've got to…
• Cycle 400 km. • Go for a 12-hour kayak in the rain. • Climb a mountain.
• Slide down cliffs on a rope.
• Toss a caber (that means throwing a log to all you non-Scots).
• And swim across a loch (that's a Scottish lake).

You've got five days to do it and you won't get much food or sleep. But cheer up, it's all in the cause of science!

Wanna sign up? Hmm – the only marathon I'm up for is a marathon pizza pig-out! But if the Third and Second Prizes seem hard to bear, the First Prize is not only hard to bear – it's hard for BEARS too! Yes – the First Prize goes to inventor Troy Hurtubise of Ontario, Canada, and his amazing bear-proof suit of armour…

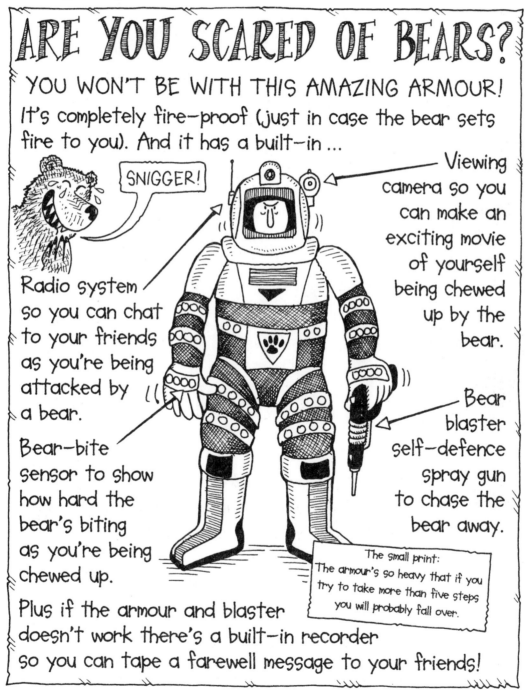

ARE YOU SCARED OF BEARS?

YOU WON'T BE WITH THIS AMAZING ARMOUR!

It's completely fire-proof (just in case the bear sets fire to you). And it has a built-in …

SNIGGER!

Viewing camera so you can make an exciting movie of yourself being chewed up by the bear.

Radio system so you can chat to your friends as you're being attacked by a bear.

Bear-bite sensor to show how hard the bear's biting as you're being chewed up.

Bear blaster self-defence spray gun to chase the bear away.

The small print: The armour's so heavy that if you try to take more than five steps you will probably fall over.

Plus if the armour and blaster doesn't work there's a built-in recorder so you can tape a farewell message to your friends!

Not only did Troy spend all his money on his bear-proof suit of armour, he also wore it for some terribly tough tests. He was…

• RUN OVER by a truck EIGHTEEN times.

• SHOT by a rifle.

• HIT by arrows.

• SMASHED by a tree trunk.

• BEATEN UP by some alarmingly large bullies armed with big bits of wood, and then he…

• JUMPED OFF A CLIFF (once).

And that, in the view of the judges, is what science is all about – trying rotten experiments and taking ridiculous risks to find out more about a mystery. Even if you don't find out that much. And come to think of it, that's what this book's been about too. Without rotten experiments, science would be far more boring and a lot less fun.

Well, that's my excuse – and I'm sticking to it!

HAPPY HORRIBLE SCIENCE, EVERYONE!